NEAR-LIFE EXPERIENCE

Rowland Bagnall's first collection, *A Few Interiors*, was published by Carcanet in 2019. His poetry, reviews and essays have appeared in *Poetry London*, *PN Review*, *The Art Newspaper* and elsewhere. He lives and works in Oxford.

NEAR-LIFE EXPER-IENCE

ROWLAND BAGNALL

CARCANET POETRY

First published in Great Britain in 2024 by
Carcanet
Alliance House, 30 Cross Street
Manchester, M2 7AQ
www.carcanet.co.uk

A CIP catalogue record for this book is
available from the British Library.

ISBN 978 1 80017 390 3

Book design by Andrew Latimer, Carcanet
Typesetting by LiteBook Prepress Services
Printed in Great Britain by SRP Ltd, Exeter, Devon

The publisher acknowledges financial
assistance from Arts Council England.

CONTENTS

FOR BECKY
for teaching me to pay attention

What does the hard look do to what it sees?
Pull beauty out of it, or stare it in?
— Denise Riley, 'Outside from the Start'

Well I used to be sort of blind
Now I can sort of see
— Bill Callahan, 'Rococo Zephyr'

NEAR-LIFE EXPERIENCE

NOTHING PERSONAL

The century surges,
shuddering on, accelerating in pursuit
of someplace rumoured up ahead, swallowing

dusk after dusk of wilful, uninfected time
in cold-blooded mouthfuls, growing huger
and more disarranged.

In the end isn't the point that this is all meant
to relate to us? To tell us – in a broad sense – that
the message is about ourselves?

Instead, maybe the message is that *we*
are understood by *them*, giving us a meaning
at the time we most require it.

Still, like the inhabitants of a city
soon to be razed by a unit of cavalry, know
that this is happening *in spite of* not *because of* you.

The mountains are silent, though they speak
to each other, the gold air thin at the top of them,
a flowering peak, from which point can be seen

a valley of arrivals and departures,
smouldering campsites, a bend in the river,
livestock and settlements, not an inch of land unclaimed.

THE HARE

I wake into the morning
  and find unanimous spring
  and the windows are pale with filtered light
  and the day asks, *How shall I survive myself?*
  and read a poem which ends, *let it be small enough*
  and my throat feels dry
  and the new rains have defanged the night
  and the blackthorn is over, or its blossom is
  and the lights burn blue
  and imagine a harvest and dry stacks of wheat
  and answer my e-mails in record time
  and feel deep currents of understanding
  to find a living mosaic, polished and repetitive
  smothering the yellow dawn
  and the white sky is canoeing south
  and have certain phrases in my head, including *silent stroboscopic waves*
  and see ghosts and know that one of them is Robert Frost
  and consume a pear from Argentina
  and take in the general feel of the place
  fading like a set of tracks
  and write *I wake into the morning / and find unanimous spring*
  and pass my hand through my own body
  and feel omnipresent cloaks of rain
  and the oceans appear silvery
  which is stabbing into months of ice
  and think *what kind of poet writes* 'I wake into the morning / and
   find unanimous spring'?
  and the harvesters are lying down, taking a rest
  and its knowable sequence
  and it caverns
  and it opens like an eyelid
  and it stalks us as you stalk a hare

NEAR-LIFE EXPERIENCE

So far the year is imprecise,
spelling itself out using a limited vocabulary.

Outside it is greys and browns and dark, rich, spruce-hued greens,
life, or very close to life, the wind whipping in twos and threes,
rain seeking us out.

I test the coffee and the coffee table, which seem
real enough, as does the eucalyptus tree I've noticed only
just now after many months.

Acre-hungry fires are licking the outback,
exposing giant sketches on the surface of the earth: an eye, a hand,
a mouth starting to speak.

Everything looks futuristic, as though it hasn't really happened yet
or like it's only just pretending to have happened and will
suddenly switch on 'for real'.

The pure contralto still sings in the organ loft;
the mate is always ready with his lance and his harpoon.

Liz is hunting rabbits in Wisconsin;
Adam is bowing his head during *The Burial at Ornans* (1849-50),
inhaling luminously painted air;
Becky turns her head in Miró's studio in Palma;
Stephen, Jane, and Ariel are sleeping now in Montreal.

The grasslands here have all grown back.
The grey waters recede.

I delete myself, returning to a previous save-point.

When I arrive, so light I can barely move – loopholes, static, terrible
slaughters – the situation hastens, veering about, and the wind whips past
   again
cutting my younger, cleaner, stranger face.

FREIGHTER

How much can it
take – the level evening
and its centre like a season
shifting gear?

Hardly any time
has passed – is it just me, or
is it just me that's getting this?
The bait-and-switch
of the dying light,
the unfinished business
of the waves, the feeling
something's missing – and I mean
really missing.

On the mainland,
now radiating some of
its great strength – granite,
breccia, hornblende
schist – best understood
in motion – you can feel the tilting
of the earth.

A few miles
down the coast a town has lost
its people, proving
nothing – or nothing yet.

Can you hear
the susurration of the headland?
See the insanely circular movement
of the gulls?

And this is what the poem
is like – the shape of a room
and the objects in it
scattering like fish – arriving
into somewhere else, dragooning us
along with it – a pendulum
distributing its weight – like sailing into secret
waters, different when remembered –
and disembarking nimbly
somehow here and now refreshed.

DOUBLE VISION AT THE SINK

Every time you're looking out you're really / looking in
                           – lines removed from the poem

Today I'm looking down into a white ceramic sink,
         the water running coldly and opaquely
from the tap: my task is shelling jumbo shrimp,
         snapping the carapace away, slipping my index
finger in beneath the lightly cracking exoskeleton
         to peel the interlocking segments of the abdomen
apart, the empty casings piling up like shavings
         from a wooden bowl. I try to think of looking
down as looking out into the sky, receding as you reach it
         as if desperate to get somewhere. Across
its face I see a shimmering man, winking and smiling.
         I witness his intrusion and acknowledge it,
watching his limbs become translucent, ultimately
         wasting to a single point of greenish light.
That afternoon we'd been up at the Cloisters, which
         I hadn't known was where they keep the so-called
Mérode Altarpiece (c.1428): in it the Annunciation takes
         place in a private room, a simple, square
domestic space, furnished unassumingly, at least until
         the objects come to stand for something
else, as in the just-extinguished candle or the table,
         which has sixteen sides. To the right of this
is Joseph, drilling holes into a piece of wood. Behind
         him is a street-scene of a European
town, outdating him by something close to
         fourteen hundred years. In the pale base
of the sink I see what looks to be a tapestry.
         Everything is foreground: the chase, the capture,
the imprisonment, the cheeky crowds of onlookers
         – dressed lavishly, I'd say, even for them –
an instantaneous parade of different cloths

and coloured silks, intricately woven
by the makers of the scene, in which the hunters
        seem to run as if they had no weight at all.
I develop a talent for identifying symbolism,
        seeing it everywhere in fruits and flowers
and hand gestures in photographs, in insects, rodents,
        and varieties of birds, in the camouflage
of reptiles, plane trees, and specific moths, the touch
        lamp on the bedside table, the heat from
the oven, even in the bowl of glossy, naked, blue-grey
        shrimp, which stand for something like fragility
or time or the unknowable. Another layer of snow,
        mid-week. Another tapestry beneath the first,
this one showing the miraculous revival of a man
        who very nearly died. A woman on the sidelines
holds what looks to be a piece of glass. A second
        figure fades into the lush textural scenery.
Three or four days on, I chart the progress of our
        journey on a small tiltable screen,
embedded in the headrest of the window seat
        in front of me. The screen offers a plane's
-eye view, allowing me to gaze down on the plane
        in which we're travelling. The crew switch
on the cabin's artificial night, induced by deep
        fluorescent strips running the whole length
of the fuselage. The planet is divided into time zones
        on a gridded map. I zoom in on the country
then the city we've just left, then the apartment,
        then the kitchen where I see myself before
the sink, my fingers working neatly on the silvery-grey
        shrimp, the sink's shimmering surface pale,
more or less reflecting me, winking and smiling,
        looking out into the room like looking
down into the opaque non-reflection of the sky.

EIGHT STUDIES OF A HAND

The image deepens and solidifies,
becoming almost memory.
I see the fingers and think *fingers*.
I see the wrists and say to myself *wrists, wrists*,
as if with superstition (which I won't go into now).

The skin starts to emit its own unusual blaze.
I experience what feels like an exposure
to the obviously waxy quality of time,
considering the steady restoration
of a building and its furniture.

Yesterday we drove out to the Suffolk coast
and watched our friend bury his face in stones.
My hands, during this time, appeared increasingly
unlike my own, the way that basic truths
about yourself can come to sound

entirely unreasonable. On the drive home
I thought about a moment I remembered from
The Grapes of Wrath (1939), in which
a nameless woman laughs to find
she's had part of her hand shot off,

a chuckling hysteria in her throat that grew
louder and higher with each breath,
her shattered hand – *a hand which had*
no knuckles – appearing to me as it
would've appeared to her family

decades later: frail and unsatisfied,
pitifully underused. September's rolling
slowly in. I feel certain of my own name,
of the resistance of the brake pedal,
of feeling drawn on by a force that feels

a bit like magnetism, dragging us
ahead to somewhere no one can be
sure about. And that's what seems to be
the thought of Lange's migrating labourer,
whose hands are scarred and carved

out of the very wood he's leaning on,
as if you could stop and read his whole life
from the creases of his open palm
or even tell him what the future holds
before he grasps and handles it.

THE SURE SEASON

This morning we were struck
by frost: new crispness, solid underfoot,
more blue, really, than silver, each
leaf and blade of grass held fast,
hoping to melt (using the sun) to life.

It doesn't take a lot to find
that everything looks out of place, newly disturbed,
unreturnable, perhaps, to how
you remember it.

Here lacks the certainty
of mountain ranges, wise in their similarity,
or the jagged crashing of the coastline, which at least
everyone knows is changing – the sea eating
the land like acid, the bone grip of the cliffs
occasionally loosening, revealing
a new shelf of fossils.

I used to think that every day
the world stayed pretty much the same
but *you* woke up a little different. For a while, I felt
the opposite: that I was me, all of the time, and seasons
shed the world like skin, proof of their growth –
just as volcanoes, tree rings, even dust are
proof of something being made.

Now I think a blend of these – or quickly
change my mind between them so that both appear
true at once, like a nineteenth century illusion
where two separate illustrations can be merged
by twiddling a string: bird and cage, horse and rider.

This reminds me of the first time
that I drove home through a snowstorm, early December,
two-thousand-and-something, snow falling in uneven
clumps – accumulation and erasure – the road
quietly vanishing, no sign of resistance.

KNOWN UNKNOWNS

Unobserved, I pot
            these weightless seeds
in compost – hurling something at
            the future, like making it happen.

Some are fang-shaped,
            others orbed – the eyes
of tiny fish swimming now
            blindly out of sight, still living.

Is this what you might call
            a lyric situation, a moment
like a giant wave that
            seems to have predicted you?

*The difficult thing is to prove
            what one believes*: insect casings,
almonds, grass; your question, *Trees* –
            your answer, also *Trees*.

Is this what happened
            when a child I knew said
Music is the night awake – or was this
            something different?

Seed like a basketball,
            seed like an arrowhead – shower
of seeds raining down on a battle,
            dusting its corpses, sprouting on impact.

This is a type of knowledge, too –
        of knowing when to let yourself be
planted and watered – like being – though
        unseen – believed or believed in.

A LULL IN THE BIRDS

To the left, let's say
a country lane

The hour
begins to eat itself

No redemption
can happen to you
just like October can
happen to you

A pavement
in the end
can blossom

α

Language eclipses itself
an eye leaving its socket

Today was
like today was
in the surface of a helmet's dome

We miss
another different window

What, if anything, is
with you?

α

This accidental dance
Resolves

The time
fizzes with
autoplay

A picture of the Earth
morphs into
all times in the
future

The speaker
in the wake of things

Un-ordinary
Longish
years

α

'Tomorrow' and 'today' collide
The missteps
trips us up

For a moment
Sheer
ongoing changes

Meaning has
a kind of
form

α

Continue together

Elisions and
a three-way street

No flowers
can happen to you
just like eye contact can
happen to you

If we have to disappear
we can

VIEWS OF THE WINTER (NOVEMBER 1899)
for AH

I

because it is winter,
because the yellow afternoon is short,
because the grass can't move as it wants to,
because the crowds around the pool have stopped,
because you can still feel the night's residual cool in the earth,
because the dirt hems their cloaks,
because it has happened,
because it is happening,
because the light skims at the edge of things,
because the new wet low sky pinks,
because the water petitions you, calling you out,
because the darkness wants to know where you go each day,
because the colours break their surfaces,
because this scheme of things is fixed,

I

because it is winter,
because it strips the park in sheets,
because the people are strolling, controlling the atmosphere,
because the trees are shielding trees,
because you have a thought and feel it,
because your inattention jolts,
because water is one way and sun is another,
because it punctuates the earth,
because this all takes up its place again a century ahead of you,
because the upper branches merge,
because if you think about it nothing that much has changed,
because you see it seeing you,
because it is happening,
because it stands to happen soon,

FEELING AND PAINTING

If you look closely at the hunters
in *The Hunters in the Snow* (1565)
you'll see the slight translucent aspect
of the central figure's head, which seems to let an outline
of the deep-set winter tree trunk through.

It makes me think he's fading very slowly from the scene,
that in another five hundred years or so
only his footprints will be left, that his companions
won't have clocked he's gone or even recognise his name
when later questioned of his whereabouts.

I like to imagine him materialising into the stable world
of other paintings, phasing into contexts that he doesn't have
the knowledge or the language to describe. Lately I've seen him
in *The Avenue at Middelharnis* (1689), walking alone
between the not quite parallel lines of the trees

beneath a sky that seems both day and night,
as if time in the picture were somehow getting ahead of itself.
And between the paintings I imagine | warping and assimilating
lights, the | microbial jungling of | colours
          | splintering the tide | like foliage

| leaving an image there | like foliage behind your
     | crashing down behind your
                    | eyes
| then shifting | yes, but no rain
        | and a slight | bend in the

                                    | superimposition
| of the trees | an entirely mosaicked
                              | planetary light
      | pushing the | cloudy, yes, but no rain
| into | drastically   foreshortened

      | life | which lets an outline of
                     | both day and night
| into the stable | not
          | mosaicked | lines of | slight translucent
| fading | sky | cloudy, yes, but no rain, though it's coming,

          | crashing down behind your | image there
of | footprints | phasing into | snow
| getting ahead of itself | to let an outline
of | his whereabouts | appear like foliage
beneath the trees. Back in the Brueghel painting,

beyond the black cross of a bird preserved
in low mid-flight – the only thing existing in the deep space
of the painting's frame – the villagers are skating
in the valley on the frozen lakes. In the distance
is another village or the same village

repeated with its own returning hunters looking
back across the view to us: another pack of hungry
dogs, another bonfire kicking in the wind, another
oblivious community, making the most of it,
another disappearing man. I've been here,

somehow, to this other place. And I have been
that bird, witnessing a scene that both rejects you
and invites you in, repeating to myself along
an avenue of trees: *Under the skates: ice.*
Under the ice: apparently the sky.

SHATTERED IN FALL

That sword is sad and beautiful and, / This visionary cave
— machine learning algorithm

Should we have seen that coming? Should we have seen that weird terrific scenery, silent and often not silent, rising high with multi-coloured curvature and stones? I'm being present in this landscape, an upward-sloping maze of little arches and depressions, staying the winter, with woods that loom and thin back out, scissoring down from level to level as if branching in reverse. Meanwhile: air-conditioned rooms; a jug of just-in-season flowers; a book on which I see the words *ecstatic* and *Detroit,* as in 'Don't you feel ecstatic to be visiting Detroit?' *Repair your ship from beneath your ship. Don't you prefer dismantled art to art?* What life there is is out of sight and quietly commingling, entirely aware of us, hypnotic though invisible, though invisibly moving, which is key: we sense it more than anything, like reading and discovering a hidden communality, the same day lived from opposite ends at a similar speed, inhaling and exhaling at once, mid-season, which is completely understandable, if only understandable in part, the way the images you picture never seem to picture you

THE CITIZENS

There used to be an image here, or not so much
an image as the first few muddled outlines of a scene,
encompassing a range of different timescales, lives and geographies,
and maybe something comes of it and maybe it doesn't,

but really it's the fact that there's a known amount of uncaptured
activity around – the kind of stuff that tends to go especially
unnoticed, like the slow work of the gardener who takes immense
care with the trees – although exactly who this tragedy belongs to

is really anyone's guess. So much has changed since then, for me:
perhaps it doesn't matter if the scratches find a form or not;
it's just you have to wait until you've seen them to have
seen them. In a play I saw a while ago, the citizens conspire

to erase themselves completely, disappearing street by street
by methods which remain unclear. Towards the end of the final act,
the play falls open like the two halves of a piece of fruit, essentially identical,
the one half near-enough intact, the other half intact, though bruised.

The world occurs to me.
I feel my way into the space and cooling air
outside, leaving behind an article about
a bridge collapse in Genoa, a city I once visited,
the sun now (relatively speaking) level with the upstairs
windows, slumping down and to the right.

I destroy my house and everything in it. I crack out
thirty ice cubes from the ice tray to the sink, return the ice tray
to the freezer and then entirely destroy the freezer.

Later on the house is fine, repaired while we were out buying
whatever. I run my hands across the table's grain, feeling
its coolness underneath my palms. When you're asleep
I come downstairs and stay up doing this for hours
for reasons which will sound insane.

At some point it becomes midday:
I study the asparagus fern, admiring the way each frond
is just another fern in miniature, immaculately detailed,
vanishingly small. But why should what I'm seeing
now be interesting to me at all? What about yesterday,
or the day before, or gearing up and planning for
whichever trip we're taking next? (Mexico City?
Back to Greece?) So what the grass is rising
after all that unexpected snow, or that those
partygoers seem to us so strange and otherworldly?
The worst has passed, not that it matters now.
A pattern of tilted squares emerges on the kitchen floor.

Another night I dreamt I went the opposite of blind,
which was to suffer an excess of sight, each substance
freshly rendered with outrageous clarity, silver-outlined,
sickeningly tangible. Since then the world appears as if
reduced to its most basic parts – sky, trees, jutting rocks –
more than enough, I think, or just about.

The sun has dropped. The garden
is very still, low-key. I'm wondering how
much of this I might remember, straining to take it in,
even these ugly, overlapping clouds. I'm reminded
of a story I was told about a woman falling off
a balcony and getting up and laughing and simply
limping away, blue air darkening the corners of the house.

A WEEK IN MARCH

I cannot bite the day to the core
　　　　　　　　　　– Edward Thomas

How does the day remember itself?
A payload of activity
braiding together – catkins,
nettles, long gradients of shape and shade.

The winter seemed like it had more to say
this year, though it'll have to wait.

The spring's already slingshotting around,
moving the furniture from room to room.

It makes me think about a house
that could turn out to be the house
in an American novel: screen door, porch,
consumptive child.

In the next chapter, a neighbour
no one really knows decides to leave
and not come back.

　　　　　　　α

Everything's returning, Champ, but
where's it all returning from?

The river hammers silver sheets.
The buds seem acupunctural.

I'm learning there are rules and then
exceptions to the rules.

Just so you know: in my head
it is Iceland and snowing hard.

α

I spend an hour thinking, *The afternoons,
are they giving or taking more?*
watching a shadow slide its way across
the floorboards to my wooden chair.

After this I read a story by Lydia Davis,
which is like peering into someone's garden
and feeling several types of jealousy at the same time.

Then I check the meanings of the following words:
hearing, seeing, backcloth, prose – imagining
a battle scene involving chariots
and naked men.

α

Tomorrow there's a polar wind,
whatever that might mean for us.

The morning comes in widescreen – roll credits.
Even the air knows to inhale itself.

I sit for a long while at my computer screen.
Eventually I write *and the rain feels cool / and the rain is cool,*
although there isn't rain.

In the next chapter, I return after many years
to find that nobody remembers me,
not even my kids, who understand me
to be a violent stranger.

α

The wind flattens the plants outside.

I read the final acts of *Titus Andronicus* (c.1592)
and again am saddest for the pigeon-keeper,
who always dies feeling confused.

Night blooms like an olive tree –
I dream I'm trekking through a country
part-way through a civil war.

α

One evening soon, I'll think about myself
this week, like having it all back again:
not the time, exactly, but the shape of it,
the way a piece of music or a sentence has a shape.

The wind retreats –
we behold the smooth wealth of the coming year,
all ornaments and bracelets.

Finally the rain comes, and the rain feels cool
and the rain is cool.

THE RIVER MORE THAN EVER

I am filled with all things seen / for the last time
   – Linda Gregg

A page has turned – been folded over. The week like a gigantic
sentence – narrow and self-unravelling – spilling with a kind of motion,
cutting, like a knife, the year. Nobody's shown. A rustling of pines, like pines hundreds
of years ago – some of them, in fact, the same, though thicker and (of course) more rooted.

Imagine turning up here now – too late, perhaps,
or much too soon – and trying to figure out what happened:
a scene made up entirely of touches and impressions, though nothing that
you might call *tangible*. Perhaps you think it's best this way – perhaps even more realistic.

The river occurs – is held by the country. Funny how it's always
moving but from up here looks completely fixed – the way moments
of stillness feel – or grief, or sleep – in life, which seem to be composed of nothing
but in fact are always on the move – like what exactly? Growth? The weather? Thinking? Little
   rushing birds?

POEM WITH RICHARD DIEBENKORN

Why is it that
this field, for example, fuzzy
and scribbled in, or the cupcake
icing of each
bungalow, reminds
me of a corridor – the kind
that seems
a metaphor for
something (though this often
happens, the mind
moving itself) – the
heat blurring the edges
of the roof tiles and the summer grass,
pine trees generating needles
in their tens of thousands, forming
cones, the sun making
its slow way
out, recorded in
the colour of the tarmac and the
bursting leaves?

Shirtless, maybe, brush
in hand, I summon
Richard
Diebenkorn, measuring
the distance from his rooftop
to the beach,
narrowing his eyes
to try and pick out the horizon, the
day shrugging its shoulders, forcing in

an evening which has
already begun
elsewhere.

I think about
the year to come – picturing it running
through to
August, autumn, Halloween –
until eventually
it's out of sight, a long uneven desert road,
dissolving up
ahead into a sky
-creating
haze.

Turning back now,
Richard
speaks – *There's more time. Do you*
need it? – his
voice bringing the night
air, rushing out to the Pacific, a hum
of electricity
left crackling for many miles.

and tomorrow the same
and then still the same
and then not. I detect a slip
between seasons, from autumn
to another, less-full kind of autumn,
still humming with a loose control
as if to stave off the inevitable.
What I mean to say is, for the most part
you see nothing: a clueless sky, a shadow
thickening the walls, an all but empty
street that seems to widen to include you.
And here's the creak of branches against
other branches. And here's a well-proportioned
view of the whole town, resting silently
at night, waiting for us. Come on and
feel precise. Come on and feel this
CGI-style rain, falling in unnumbered
threads, and the Impressionist rustling
of the leaves as you pass over them,
as in a short dream of a forest floor
you'll certainly forget. I equip a battered
leather shield. The skateboarders begin
to glow. Beneath my window is
a heavy vase of scentless artificial
flowers, amazingly lifelike, and behind
them the street, in which whatever
light there is seems of the shallow
underwater kind. Why so many white
Toyotas? Is there anything Rembrandt
didn't know? While we're at it: what's with
all these particles of soon-to-be extinguished

air, shimmering like cells viewed through
an optical device? They live in one sun, we
in another, pressing the glass as if to whisper,
*That's right, when we go, we're taking you
with us.* I sense a gentle phasing out.
I imagine a body pulling its history from
the ground, examining each strand as if with
shaky recognition. You get the picture: crammed
with imperfections but in its own way beautiful,
staggering even, like an unspecified canopy,
stretching out for miles into the adjective-resistant dark.

LYNCEUS

It's here already:
moisture, light, pale sun on the house fronts –
shallow mackerel scrapes of cloud.

The visible stays visible. It seems to clarify
itself – lush meadows and woodlands,
yellow lichen on the stones.

I take stock of the weather,
see the quick facts of the racing birds –
not touching, but close – then blink

to find the names for things
now chiselled to their surfaces – *BONE,
LEAD, ACORN, SHADE* – like damaged skin.

And then a kind of glassiness, a deep strain
in my open eyes: odd streaks and beams
baptising the shape of things – bright

sheens and halations – shoals of crystal
-coloured light. It all appears, revealing
its underside – true, but only true for me.

When you see it it changes you.
It changes itself. The words you try to reach
for and their definitions fail.

It flows like blood – rushing and pulsing.
You feel alone and far away. And when
it melts – abruptly, like sun moving

behind the clouds – you stay changed
and a voice sings, *Are you known here?*
Do you want to be?

AN ATLAS

It's summer
around us, a
picture we're
living in, as
though living
were a substance
that could ease
out like a taken
breath – the same
breath you are
taking now,
drifting your
slow way
through lakes
of experience,
crushing up
at last against
tomorrow
which is
like today.

Time happens
here in hills
and slopes,
increments of
everything de
-caying in soft
sequences –
replaced at
once invisibly
by sequences

ahead – though
everything that's
seen from here
absorbs you
like a leaf
the sun.

Eventually it's
just a case of
how long you
go on for,
two hands
writing side
by side down
two halves of
an empty
page, one
producing
what it sees,
the other what
it thinks about,
reacting in re
-sponse to sight
like blossom
flipping from
the trees.

And so, the scene
abandons you,
the new
afternoon
now describing
itself, its colours
and connectedness,

the sun proposing
no alternative
to the way
that things are
playing out,
faster and faster,
believe it
or not, summer,
winter, winter,
spring.

CONFIRM HUMANITY

Sitting in a square in
Europe – coffee and tables,
small child in a
puffer jacket.

It's good for a city
to build around water – the coast
and other knife-like edges,
a series of canals and rivers.

I saw a man
preparing gooseberries
in a kitchen
through a ground floor window.

I imagine – in some
detail – his hands holding
the paring knife: knuckles,
wooden handle, blade.

A couple
cross the square
in sunglasses
of uncertain ironicness.

There are planters
where I'm sitting
but whatever grew inside
them's died.

I think about a scene from
Train Dreams (2011),
a scene I can't seem
to forget about.

It knows – I think –
that ghosts are more
a presence than
an absence,

that haunting's
what we've always
wanted and – in many ways –
have always had.

Apparently, Matisse
once went to see
the aging,
arthritic Renoir,

moved to find him
painting with
a brush
tied to his fingers.

Two trees
growing side-by-side
have branches
that are making contact – as if

in friendship, curiosity
– another body, similar but not
my own – something to touch, a thing
that knows me.

All this is a ghost: big sky, big land, big feeling of being
here. Wind in the grasses. Ridges and fields. Rain-washed trees and
non-trees. What business is the dawn of mine? now crushed by
the weight of it, feeling not myself, exactly, though not
not myself – the same thing in a newer way – the snowman's great abstractions. Yon
cursor lingers o'er the face of a seventeenth century serving maid. An oaken
table drenched in flowers. Water jugs and loaves of bread. A goldfinch on
a bowl of fruit – breathing different
air to you. *Soak up the beautiful
springtime vibes. You're free to move,
so move.* That's a palm leaf. That's the dusk. That's an
airplane over Massachusetts sounding its way through to you. Here's
a question meaning *What did you know?* and *When did you know it?*
Here's a thing you haven't named. I see a river, but
what is a river – other than
a thought that cancels everything
in front of you? Move quickly. Touch nothing.
The mornings leave themselves unmade.
Sensation in reaction. You know how it goes. Understand you
understand it – know the thaw implies the freeze. Choking out the newer shrubs
the cold makes its own silence, producing relatedness, line after
line. Great Scott, Marty! Shapelier and
shapelier – the sea cutting the flurried rocks. A beetle shining
in the sun. A billboard made of lights saying, *It happened, only
where were you?* Unforeseen and unfore-
seeable. Should we have memorized these trees? It is
what you say it is. Malformed. Incomplete. A landscape missing
mountains. We eat it and it
braces us. The taste of it. Its substance.

LANDSCAPE UNEVENNESS

In spring, when rain
that fell some days
ago has all but
evaporated, becoming purposeful humidity,
the ground gives slightly
in to you, your
feet meeting the half
resistance, a landscape unevenness.

Usually this has no
impact – is largely ignorable –
unless your movement makes
it happen, where "it"
equals everything and everything
that comes to mind,
each step bringing about
the trees, engendering clouds.

Today produced a single
muntjac – or so it
appeared – initiated by a
slip, the colour of
raw clay, emitting centuries
of heat – millennia even –
like watching myself crash
away through the brush.

Can you explain   how, like a cloak,
this water, soaking   up the minor variations
of the trees, is   spreading over what was
once in semi-tropic   fecund light? And
what about these coral-   coloured, spectral
seas, hovering an   inch above the features
of the – is it? – land?   Dusk begins its strange
descent, search   -and-destroying itself
in our direction, starting   up a point somewhere
beyond the point that   we can see, crawling
its way through to us   in modulating,
strophic waves. *What's a guy   gotta do to*
entirely regenerate   around here? What kind
of collapsing civilization   even is this? your
body swaying gently like   a body standing in
a boat. This is certainly   the place that we
set out for all those   years ago – not what
I pictured, sure, but basically   the same: same
rising hills, same   cliffs, same polygonic structures
underpinning everything. If this   were a movie,
I guess this'd be the moment   I get eaten by
a pack of dogs.   If this were a novel, this'd
surely be the   moment I quit reading the
novel, wild and   unbelievable and yet too
easy to predict the end.   I toggle between
vantage points: my own –   seeing my empty
hands – and then a full three   -sixty overview,
which shows the dusk still   brushing its way here,
coproducing new activity   that blossoms
from the outside in,   hymning the chameleon
shift of the terrain from ochre   to a reddish

– even purple? – shade,   like, not a forest exactly,
more like the idea   of a forest solidifying in
your mind.   A blue line marks our progress
on the map, blank   at the edges, as though the
countryside dissolved to mist   at some point farther
off, *a dark / Illimitable   Ocean without bound,* etc.,
a frontier which, for   now, is still closed off to you,
like thoughts   released into the night, roaming
the precincts for a place   to – like a raptor –
land. It is what   it is, as my brother would say.
Not much we can   do but feel the surf of young
night coming on, increasingly   material, the way
you hold some   objects and they suddenly feel
true. And after that,   who knows? We push on,
departing and   arriving both, watching ourselves
wading through the   oversaturated land.

SIGNS OF LIFE
https://i.ytimg.com/vi/BPba3d7KMYI/maxresdefault.jpg

Imagine encroachment.
Imagine it vanishes from the mind as it scrolls past,
awaiting comparison.

Once it starts, it's difficult to stop – something
in the way the colour reaches then horizons you, seeping beyond
itself, disequipping you of every sense.

If it were up to me, I know what I'd ask that ultimate
window, the sky, or I'd know what *not* to ask.

The water's grey.
The Netherlands are algal bloom.
What was once the San Diego River glistens like a dark blue glass.

Whither beachfront condos? Whither the beach
for that matter, its undiscovered fossil life,
more than photography?

Think *Planet of the Apes* (1968) – the waves, the sand,
that long-haired, shrivelled astronaut who died, like,
two thousand years ago.

About suffering they were never wrong, / The Old Apes…
Because I could not stop for Apes – / Apes kindly stopped for me –

You have no other option but to row yourself
to shore, your escape pod in the middle of the lake
starting to flood and sink.

LOOSE IN THE FIELD
after Mark Ford

So, the sea   The head suffers
outgrows its edges,   its images. That
these buildings at the   mossy, rain-slicked
shoreline either   boulder's getting
                    too close
or not close   for comfort,
enough.   don't you agree?

Get in there   The night comes
and walk around;   usefully to hand,
the textures are quite   like a specific, built-in
real. The wind is   quality, the moon
          keeping itself
busy, performing   to itself, both quiet
some function or other.   and unwavering.

But on the surface   Alternatively, you can
of things, there's   hear the clouds
no reason   and watch the swifts
you should understand   bombing the greasy sky, noting
          their movements
are a kind of   and their counter
dance.   -movements.

UNDER THE EQUALIZING NIGHT

A mountain stream descending to the sea.

The radiation of the snows.

Thousands of insects smashing the windscreen.

Thousands of insects not smashing the windscreen.

An uncontainable, retreating view.

A water-damaged athlete under many-angled, greenish lights.

The somewhat imaginary noises of the sea.

A woman with a horse's skull or with a rock shaped like a horse's skull.

A room of silent de Chiricos, eyeing themselves in the empty gallery.

A quarter moon cresting the Alps.

Infrared cameras monitoring temperature.

Apollinaire's lines: *I am everywhere or rather I am beginning to be everywhere.*

Hart Crane's last bear, *shot drinking in the Dakotas.*

A single horse standing in a field doing nothing.

The ongoing approach of spring.

The ongoing approach of spring.

Us travelling at close to three-hundred kilometers per hour.

Us eyeing the dawn as it absorbs into itself the night.

PROJECTIONS AND INTERSTICES

Sometimes I regret that I am not
the dying afternoon, completing in dull furrows
of fading light, level-balanced in anticipation of the evening
and its territory. Nor am I the gap between
these two adjacent, moving points, doing their best to resemble
each other, like a gap between experiences or time
you can't account for though it happened and included you.
I picture a bridge linking neighbouring countries
where the languages are similar and so is the terrain,
except the sun feels maybe stronger here
with deeper, sharper contrast and a cross-hatched shade
that baffles you, forcing you to reconsider
the relationships between things.

And yet, arriving in another place, a new landscape
of pristine hills and cities joined to other cities
by a clutch of intersecting roads, I become
not what catches sight of the world from a great height,
now floating over high white peaks, nor somebody
remembering the stages of an awkward journey,
but instead a thing of contemplation as the wind here
contemplates the trees, shaking them back and forth, sensing
their woodenness. Sometimes, also, I regret that I am not
the wind, in constant motion and unpredictable,
like a section of river into which occasionally
a fish will swim against the current
and be driven back.

THINK FAST

Light filters in.
There is a tightness in the dusk, like love.
Each day evolves beyond your need for it.
So, tell me, are you

feeling seen?

α

The rain outnumbers us.
No sign of it stopping through these hours
of unglistened night. Nothing to do but to give
yourself over. Marvel at the

squeegee dawn.

α

Same problem, same solution.
The solid-seeming water holds the mountains
like a cradled face. Drag your deer to the roadside,
splattered with headlights.

Any questions?

α

Coffee and apple juice
out on the deck. I watch the shadows leeching

colour from the bracken and the fleeting dew.
Pray, how do you

enlanguage that?

α

Fade out autumn.
Bring in winter's sleek returns.
A friend wipes ash from the hood of her car.
Horizons razorblade

to view.

α

What does your suspicion say?
Freezing waters. Mulching leaves. A sun
-bronzed cafeteria. The morning scoops light
on the sand. Nobody sees.

Go figure.

α

Total yellow. Screens of trees.
I sit at the window, through which I see
other things. I watch for them, I listen out,
and that is

the situation.

α

The meagre light remembers you,
touching up your skin-gloved hand. The weather mirrors
yesterday's. Simple and uncomplicated. Enjoy it, Pal,
while you still can. Let day's train

overrail you.

α

Funny thing is, you give it
shape and – giving shape – a meaning.
The brief reign of the frost is done.
Is it really

any wonder?

α

At last, the thick-skulled hours
retreat. What's in it for them, anyhow? The sun crowns
lightly into view, a silent transmission, and the feeling comes to you
like warmth or like an almost abstract kind

of pain.

THE NATURE OF ARRIVAL

he will / become a fine thing, perhaps, but a different one
— Jack Gilbert

He tries to refuse it: stone fields and exhausted sky,
a landscape built of repetitions. Absolute rockface,
meaningless sea – now still, now vibrating, the beginning
and the end of something. The dusk falls gracefully
apart, a building designed to be easily moved. Across
the island, stone walls split the empty hills like two sides
of a single thought. Walking back up from the beach,
remembering a time that seems now definitely over,
remembering, also, a man reaching his hand into
a bucket of discoloured squid, he feels an unknown
sense of order, dull but sharply clear, the weight of
an unusual rock. In the morning, looking out to sea,
there appears to be another island, ten or twenty miles
away, that either wasn't visible or didn't used to be there.

MID-JUNE SONATA

Early evening light appearing lately
in the garden leaves, an
ongoing influence, shredded petals taking
on the colours of a
canyon wall, the light passing
abruptly through them like a
thunderstorm that breaks from nowhere.

Time hurries in unusual ways,
a day the days begin
to shrink, as if in
retraction, exposing the continuous *away*
of things, a mode of
abandonment – endless departures – so that
even what arrives is leaving.

Have I been here all
this time or is this
something I in part imagined?
Swifts half-sleeping in the thermals,
clambering shadows, blues I don't
believe in fully – seeping as
a tide into an estuary.

This means nothing new, although
it seems completely unexpected – and
so achieves a kind of
newness, like a tree thinking
itself to leaves – each flowerhead
and bud somehow the present
and the future, simultaneously clear.

POEM FOR CHARLOTTE AND JACOB'S WEDDING

A strange goodbye, like the end of a summer,
though autumn's round the corner with a summer of its own,
inviting you to wander through its evenings and its pitching rain,
a place beyond imagination, shivering with trees.

There's light in the botanic gardens, pulsing
with a kind of life, and friendly sounds out on the street
(which are other lives too, of course) in which you play a crucial part,
like heat or the wind or the shape of the clouds, now filtering
above you like a newfound sense of clarity.

It's like a framed map on a painted wall – contours
and mountains and mountainous seas – becoming a part
of you simply by being there, adding to your memory in thin,
unnoticed increments, zone by faded, sun-washed zone – a section
of forest, a slice of the lake – until the whole thing pushes out of you,
a light source or an energy.

In the meantime, don't forget to tell yourselves that
life has architecture, too, with dust that needs sweeping
and space for new furniture, which will always be true, I think,
however full or clean it seems.

And know that there are parts of you that never really
change at all, parts you don't know about, that only others know
in you, the future floating quickly here in bright winters and coastlines,
the sweet sweat of a wood in spring, the warm airs of Connecticut
and England and Greece, Chicago and Denver, New Jersey
and New York itself, which is where you are alive today,
receiving the sun, which is how we imagine you.

UNRIPE PLUM

We've been waiting all October for this last plum
to ripen, still hard and inedible, resisting the process
or somehow refusing it. It changes colour
in the light getting weaker each day – sometimes purple,
sometimes mauve, even the dark blue that Cézanne uses
to underline his apples. The surface isn't smooth
but dented, cratered by the pressures of our forefingers and thumbs,
testing its readiness, pushing the flesh, like waiting for a corpse
to lose its rigor mortis and get up
and live. A single white shine near the stalk, taut
skin reflecting the shadowy room with me (another
shadow) in it – a mirror in a murky painting. I take in the dish –
oval, irregular, earthenware brown, hand-painted with
a single swan – fluid feathers, downward beak, the surface
of the plate almost the same shade as her
root-like feet, between a solid and a liquid somehow –
a solid muscularity – meat and feathers, organs,
blood – but also like a patch of oil, a slight swirl in the body
like the ripple in a piece of fabric. The plum's imperfect
curves rhyme with the curved edge
of the dish itself, the edge part of a wholeness
not completely comprehensible, the neck of the swan
curving down to the earth, apparently unbreakable or on the verge
of breaking like the things in Sharon Olds, where you're dealing
with the fixed or nearly fixed or nearly
broken – bones and ceramics, branches, waves, a
marriage, the body, each line as you read – as if the whole
world were composed of breaks that somehow hold it all together,
the way the planet's held together by
invisible tectonic plates.

THINGS TO COME

I'm in the bath: the water
is condensing like a deep fog in a silent film.
The book I'm reading's open at a picture of Chardin's, complete
– as usual – with an open drawer. There's even steam in the painting,
lifting slightly from a china cup.

The walls around me have been limewashed white.
I've just shaved in the mirror and decide that I look nearly dead:
my hands are biblically pale and scarred;
my eyes feel very tired.

I'm listening to Bert Jansch singing folksongs about
failing love. Outside several birds address the morning,
though it's really night, as though life
were somehow moving without going anywhere –
waiting round the corner at a place where
everything is known.

Yesterday I read a new story of Isaac's
about a woman growing up beside a family from Sicily
and about the moon landing, fifty years ago, which (on the night
they make it up there) she says feels, now, *part of my life*.

I sink my head beneath the surface, imagining
the wild night shouldering the house.

Then I imagine a map of many cities and rivers
and a columned, marble loggia – repeating itself, over and over –
a couple of saints in heavy medieval robes
floating the archways side by side. One passes
me a book, which I reach out to take;

the other wears a mask that makes him
look like many animals.

I sit for a while in the empty tub.
The music's finished, though I didn't hear it end.
When I stand my knees have soap on them and one of them
is bleeding. Apparently, it's nine o'clock.

I don't know it yet,
but tonight I'm going to wake up from a dream
that understands me back.

Sometimes I think life would be improved if we lived only once.

EPIPHANY, OR LINES FOR THE POET ON HIS THIRTIETH BIRTHDAY
simply the thing I am / Shall make me live
              – All's Well That End's Well

A cold coming you've had of it,
just the worst time of the year
for a birthday, and such a strange birthday:

Soft footfall through the parks and streets, narrow and shaded, Mediter-
ranean, the date palms and the empty fountains, *the very dead of winter.*

The bland daylight caresses you like a shoulder of hillside.

Plane trees reshadow the slick paraphrase of the grass.

At some point, not a week goes by without something shattering open
like a flower, wouldn't you say?

What is this, a Thursday?

Accept that your body has known you like the cold snap of the year has
known you, as the always-surprising woods have been known by the breeze.

Accept that sometimes in life you pass a window of uncertain sights or
pass a window of cured meats hanging like instruments; other times you
catch a glimpse of yourself in the wintery glass, threading through an
unknown place you may never return to.

There are moments when what's normal seems unlikely and miraculous,
like the daily suicides of the afternoon, and other moments when the
miracle is so mundane it disappears.

Remember to remember to remember to remember that – the common,
at-the-roadside birds moving aside, implying the sky's unimaginable edge.

What happened to the total openness of the day?

How much sherbet is too much sherbet?

but set down / This set down / This:

Not leisure, not the insincere rejoicing in the plaza,
Nor the historical thrust of the abandoned parks,
Not tedium, not the brunt adjustments of the clock,
Nor the frescoes' necessary tropes.

No, none of that.

Instead, all early evening you stabbed today into new calm, feeling per-
plexed feeling the sun go down.

How is it that you're breathing?

You used to be ten.

You used to think exactly nothing of the year yawning awake, much less
about its rain-washed streets, the refillable moon, its patches of appearing
light igniting everything around you.

Even now, what do you make of the hotels and bars? The city shifting
back to life, the people all blinking and rubbing their eyes?

Do you know what I'm asking? Will you know it eventually?

Before you consider this, make way for the travellers: three out-of-town-
ers, coming in from the desert, relieved to find their way here.

It's the least you can do, given that you were once beset like them.

The stars – if you could see them – are exploding and exploding.

ANIMAL HISTORY
for Liz Scheer

Again I'm looking out over a January afternoon,
ranged with emblems of the finished year. It conceals

nothing, establishing the first few layers of colour,
although this doesn't seem to matter now as much as

it used to, neither evidence nor a lack of evidence
of anything. A child throws a red ball on the lawn.

Behind, a blue whale yawns apart its mouth, the same
as history, which opens, gaping, to receive us.

A telegenic couple holding hands are wearing backpacks
with adjustable straps. Elsewhere, a room of identical

-seeming men dance with their eyes closed thinking,
Music? What music? as the sky turns lilac, pink,

then white and looks miraculous. Feel the texture
and you become the texture; dive into the sea

and you become the sea, zigzagging the shore
like an endangered species. It's like walking through

the many centuries of an existing landscape,
a double consciousness, witnessing the ritualistic frenzy

of each year as it goes by, accelerating past you like
a string of ornamental beads. And the animals

– damning, yes, and violent, but also beautiful and
beautifully curious – are eyeballing you carefully:

saying *snake* a snake appears, green, patterned
with triangles; up on the roof, between the lounger

and the potted palm, a woman jabs her rifle at
a curtain of approaching crows. In the same building

– or so I imagine it – a man, hunched over
on his hands and feet, finally admits everything

to himself as the walls fall flatly open and away,
the building rushing upwards like a tree

growing without constraint. On a clear day
in winter, you can see yourself down on the ground,

sussing out the difference between this year
and the next, and if it's summer, which feels less clear

each time you come back to it, the country seems more
open somehow, greater distances between the days.

UPPSALA

Eventually it's clear that we are always in
a kind of transit, forever *en route* – blinking curiously around
at all the suddenness of things we see, whether flying
over Norway's coast, unreasonably bright, wide sashes of silver water
snaking inland, or driving through the cork trees of
a burnt valley in Portugal, the ridge studded with wind turbines.
It's strange to think that someone was the first
to venture up this way, to follow these steep lines of quartz,
feeling the cold through many layers of fur. What must they
have thought of it? Why not remain? Perhaps they felt
apart, a distance, which happens fairly often now – that
things feel at a slight remove, temporarily shut off from you.
The question, badly put, is how to figure out a route
back in, to readjust to your surroundings
like recalling a lost memory. I, for example,
used to feed the same horse at the far edge of a bumpy field
and remember its eyes and the star on its nose, though
not – surprisingly – its name or whether there were any others.
Sometimes you can only hope to get to know what's
there before you, before you speed off in a new direction,
past the churches and whatever else – the river and the river's movement.

VISION OF EZEKIEL

The sky is patching.
Outside the clouds
are doing that *are we*
secretly smoke thing
they sometimes do
Their specific meanings
heavy-laden,
obviously full of weight

the frail sun
feels good and nice
just-now mounting the
horizon
in every century
an outrageously
beautiful mountainous
view

whose shape is yet to
be determined
What else was there?
teenage bathers
unimpressed by the
spectacle
the crowd making its
way back down

And what to do
about the new haze of
crispness
retooling

this part of the plain,
an   unstable   mixture
of things as they are
all   of   the   time

whatever that means
for   you.
Imagine,   as   you're
forced to in this scene,
the   unevenly
distributed weight of
the   present
A   familiar   door

pointing   out   how
language   stretches
over something it can't
quite   cover
overwhelmed by detail
announcing   itself
into   the   speaker's
mouth, not with an 'I'

but   an   'us.'
It   feels   dark   blue
I feel like if I close my
eyes   I'll   see
a   group   of   future-
holding
days
not yet embarked upon

submarining
with the promise of
anticipation
which   also   reminds

me   of   various   scenes
in   Lean's   *Doctor
Zhivago*   (1965).
and   the   snow,   it   keeps

coming   back   across   all
of   these,
a   kind   of   shorthand   for
experience.
it   "spreads"   you.
it   has   many   lives.
how   else   would
anybody   ever   notice

the   deep-ice
connection   between
things   described
[and]   other   things?
the   splendour   of
meaning
bleeding   out   of   them
at   every   turn

UNCONFORMITY AT JEDBURGH

The earth
doesn't lie. There is mud
on my boots – a young
landscape of
fences and trees,
a man whipping his leaping
horse, a phaeton keeping
up behind.
                    Grass
and open, sloping hills.

                    α

Calcareous rock – white
shellfish and chalk: the hard
presence of present things,
                    upheavals
of land.
                    My nails are grubby,
abrupt as a cutbank. My coat's
cuff has a single fray.

There will be unrest in town
and disbelief.
                    All rain
obliterates on contact.

                    α

Tilted and upright,
standing on successive
ends. We're moving
in circles – a system
of stones.
                    Once I saw
an eye change colour.
Once I watched a hoofprint
at the road's edge, in
the evening, ice.

I wonder what became
of my son, whom
I abandoned and have
never met.

Look at my shadow,
dark and oddly accurate
against the rock.

Look at my hands.

Look at my ageing skin.

THE VAST HOUR
after Genevieve Taggard

Now only is there certainty for me / When
all the day's distilled and understood – the moon
        drives at the present –
the light from here un-
        yous you.

I want to shoot myself in the face
with love – a beautiful thing in a strange
        and beautiful place. Something something
"sweet unrest" – the huge night
        an enclosure.

So stir my thoughts at this slow, solemn time –
the short-haul flights of evening: beacons of winter,
        continuous air – what if you could
read up on the day's thoughts
        about you?

Strike up music! Scope tomorrow's printless straits!
I slice the tomatoes, saving their skins – their seeds
        freckle the countertop. No ideas but in
No ideas but in things – tell me
        about it...

I stand and watch the pewter darkness. Snow
here is self-cancelling. Muscular
        planets, unread
-able moon – now *that's* what I
        call emptiness!

Cast your minds back – dredge it up: ice on
the river, mud on the trees, dataless for many miles.
      I sleep and I dream of
the previous year – and possibly (I hope)
       the next.

Now light meets darkness: now my tendrils
climb / In this vast hour – wilderness backwards,
      wilderness on. Release the hounds
of opal night, whatever you think
       that means.

This much I do know: light on the housetops,
alluvial plains, the old heart and its loyalties.
      And the evening disa
-ppearing – first the ending, now
       the end.

'Eight Studies of a Hand' quotes from *The Grapes of Wrath* and refers to Dorothea Lange's *Migratory Cotton Picker, Eloy, Arizona* (1940).

'Poem with Richard Diebenkorn': Richard Diebenkorn (1922–1993) was an American painter who lived and worked in California.

'Lynceus': In Greek mythology, Lynceus of Messene was said to possess a heightened sense of sight. As well as seeing clearly in the dark, he is occasionally described as having the ability to see through solid surfaces, including the earth.

'Confirm Humanity': *Train Dreams* is by Denis Johnson (1949–2017).

'Loose in the Field' borrows the form of Mark Ford's poem 'Then She Said She Had to Go'.

'Poem for Charlotte and Jacob's Wedding' was written to celebrate the marriage of Charlotte Crowe and Jacob Segal (September 18th, 2021).

'Epiphany, or Lines for the Poet on His Thirtieth Birthday' makes use of T. S. Eliot's 'Journey of the Magi' and owes a debt to Graham Foust's poem 'To Graham Foust on the Morning of His Fortieth Birthday'. I was born on Epiphany (6th January).

'Animal History' was written in response to a collection of paintings by Liz Scheer: https://www.lizscheer.com/animal-history.html

'Vision of Ezekiel' borrows its title from a painting by David Bomberg (1890–1957). The poem is constructed from bits and pieces of correspondence/criticism about the other poems in this collection.

'Unconformity at Jedburgh' owes something to John Clerk's 1787 illustration of geological unconformity on the banks of Jed Water in Scotland. The poem is written in the voice/mind of Scottish geologist James Hutton (1726–1797).

ACKNOWLEDGEMENTS

I'm grateful to the editors of the following publications, where several of these poems first appeared: *Action, Spectacle, Ad Alta: the Birmingham Journal of Literature, Anthropocene, bath magg, Blackbox Manifold, The Brooklyn Review, The Irish Times, The Manchester Review, The Moth, Moveable Type, Oxford Poetry, PN Review, PROTOTYPE 3* and *The Rialto*.

Writing poetry, it turns out, is more collaborative than solitary. The poems in this book would not exist – or would be far worse – without the care and demand of the following people, whose fingerprints are everywhere: Luke Allan, Matthew Bevis, Joe Carrick-Varty, Charlotte Crowe, Chloe Currens, Dominic Hand, Oli Hazzard, Adam Heardman, Isaac Nowell, Samuel Reilly, Stephen Ross, Liz Scheer, Laura Scott, James Stanfield, Eliza Tewson, Vala Thorodds and Rob Yates. Thank you all for reading and appearing in these poems.

This book was written under the supervision of Luke Kennard and Isabel Galleymore, who led me through a PhD in Creative Writing at the University of Birmingham. I will always be grateful for their generosity and friendship, and to the College of Arts and Law at Birmingham for awarding me a doctoral scholarship.

Special thanks to my family and friends, who never make me feel I should be doing something else – a powerful gift. And to Becky, my first and best reader: thank you for shaping the coasts of my life and for encouraging these poems with such intelligence and humour – what's good in them has come from you, especially the swifts and oceans.

Further thanks to Michael Schmidt and John McAuliffe, and to Mariota Spens for her extraordinary painting, which seems to understand so much.